Our Lady and the New Evangelisation

by
Donal Anthony Foley

All booklets are published thanks to the generous support of the members of the Catholic Truth Society

CATHOLIC TRUTH SOCIETY
PUBLISHERS TO THE HOLY SEE

Contents

 First published 2015 by The Incorporated Catholic Truth Society, 40-46 Harleyford Road London SE11 5AY Tel: 020 7640 0042 Fax: 020 7640 0046.

ISBN 978 1 78469 073 1

Foreword

I am delighted to see this new booklet on Our Lady and the New Evangelisation. It captures beautifully, and succinctly, her essential place in the mission of the Church. It is from Mary that the Church learns true discipleship. For this reason, Our Lady has been given the title, 'Star of the New Evangelisation'.

Under her protection, we learn how to encounter the Lord Jesus more deeply, in prayer, in meditating on the Rosary, and in being led by her into a deeper love for him and his Church. With her guidance we accompany others in their discovery of him. We help them to realise that they are called to be part, not of an Institution, but a family which has a loving Mother who cares for all her children.

I hope that many will be inspired by this booklet to draw close to Our Lady, to discover her Motherly patronage anew. May she intercede for us all. Through her Immaculate Heart, may she help us all to invite others to know and experience the loving and merciful heart of her Son, Jesus Christ.

Bishop Mark O'Toole (Plymouth)
Chair of the Bishops' Conference Department for Evangelisation and Catechesis.

Introduction

This booklet looks at the role of Our Lady in the New Evangelisation, that "missionary" outreach which recent popes have emphasised as being crucial to the Church's role in the modern world. Of course, the Church has been involved in evangelisation for the past two thousand years, ever since Christ, at his Ascension, gave his commandment to the apostles to "go and make disciples of all nations," (*Mt* 28:19). But the principle of a New Evangelisation has assumed a greater urgency since the Second Vatican Council, given that society as a whole has undergone such tremendous changes in recent years, not all of them positive, while the Church has struggled to make the message of Christ known in an increasingly hostile atmosphere.

To understand the Marian dimension of the New Evangelisation, it will be necessary for us initially to look back at the crucial role of Our Lady in evangelisation in the early Church and during the medieval period. Then we will look at the major Marian apparitions, in order to appreciate how important these were for building up the Church, before assessing the role of the modern popes in promoting both devotion to the Blessed Virgin Mary and the New Evangelisation.

Our Lady and Evangelisation in the Early Church and the Middle Ages

The New Evangelisation

The word "evangelisation" comes from the Greek, and means announcing good news, in this case the Gospel of Jesus Christ, whether to people who have not heard of it before, or to those who need to be re-evangelised. In reality, evangelisation is something every baptised Catholic should be doing, that is, reaching out to others in the name of Jesus, and proclaiming his saving message by their lives as much as by words. So evangelisation includes both befriending people and caring for their needs, while also sharing the Gospel with them with a view to their conversion.

What the New Evangelisation is

As for the New Evangelisation, this is the whole programme enacted by the Church, in various ways, from the latter part of the twentieth century onwards: the great movement to mobilise the Church for the evangelisation of the world in the third millennium in which we are now living. But "evangelisation" is not just a question of missionary activity, but also encompasses re-evangelising those cultures where Christian influence has diminished, and also looking at the way that Catholic thought and practice can act as a "leaven" in improving society in a moral and cultural sense, as indicated in the parable of the leaven (*Mt* 13:33).

In September 2010, Pope Benedict XVI issued a *motu proprio* apostolic letter, *Ubicumque et Semper*, establishing the Pontifical Council for Promoting New Evangelisation. In this, he stated that "the mission of evangelisation, a continuation of the work desired by the Lord Jesus, is necessary for the Church: it cannot be overlooked; it is an expression of her very nature." He also noted that the New Evangelisation requires a "constant interior renewal, a continuous passing, so to speak, from evangelised to evangelising," that is, that the Church needs to be renewed in an interior sense before it can successfully go out to the world.

Our Lady and the New Evangelisation

As will become clear in the course of this booklet, devotion to the Blessed Virgin had a very important role during the first evangelisation of the cultures of antiquity, and this continued and deepened during the medieval period, when devotion to her was very widespread. Likewise, we will see how, after the Reformation, Our Lady was very important in the process of re-establishing Christianity as a force in society following the break-up of Christendom. In the more modern era, too, through her approved apparitions, she has been of great importance in strengthening the Church, and thus it can be argued that her role in the New Evangelisation must also be promoted and understood if this evangelisation is to be truly fruitful.

To understand why Our Lady has traditionally been so highly venerated in the Church, though, it is necessary to look back over two thousand years of Church history. Hence this booklet will devote space to a necessary consideration of what has gone before, both in terms of the Blessed Virgin's importance in theological and historical terms, and also her role in evangelisation in the past.

Our Lady in the Gospels

The Blessed Virgin has a crucial place in the Gospels, but devotion to her didn't cease at that point, and even from the earliest days we find evidence of this in the writings of the Church Fathers - the important early Christian writers and teachers - particularly when they described her as the "New Eve". The implication of this term was that she was in partnership with the "New Adam". Christ, and that just as Eve caused Adam to sin when they stood before the Tree of Life in the Garden of Eden, and thus helped to drag down the human race (*Gn* 3), so Our Lady, by co-operating with Christ in our redemption, helped to raise up mankind.

She did this particularly at the crucifixion, when she stood at the foot of the cross, the new "tree of life," and offered herself with her Son in his redemptive sacrificial death for all mankind, as he conferred on her the role of Mother of the Church and of all believers (*Jn* 19:26-27). But her role clearly went right back to the Incarnation and birth of Christ, and even before that, so the Church teaches, to her Immaculate Conception in the womb of her mother, St Anne. This was the privilege of her being conceived without original sin, which of itself puts the Blessed Virgin in a unique category, and one which prepared her for her role as Christ's mother. That fact, on its own, clearly indicates the extraordinary importance of her role in the economy of salvation, but her position in subsequent Catholic history was also vital.

Devotion to Our Lady in the Early Church

After her Assumption into heaven, which, like the Immaculate Conception, is now a defined dogma of the Church, we can assume that there certainly was devotion to Our Lady in the early Church, during the first three hundred years of its existence when it underwent severe persecutions. These persecutions, though, may have inhibited such devotion, and another factor may have been the idolatrous nature of religion at the time, with its focus on gods and goddesses. There was a real danger of Mary being taken for a "goddess", and thus impeding the spread of a doctrinally orthodox Christianity. But when the persecutions ceased, and the influence of idolatry and paganism had diminished, then devotion to the Blessed

Virgin blossomed marvellously, indicating that she had an important role in evangelising at the time.

We can see this in the proclamation of her as the *Theotokos*, the God-bearer, at the Council of Ephesus in AD 431. This pivotal proclamation involved a belief in Jesus's true human nature, while at the same time safeguarding belief in his divinity, such that in the hypostatic union between the divine and human natures of Christ, he was both Son of God and Son of Mary.

Even before that, though, we have evidence of practical Marian devotion in the prayer *Sub tuum praesidium*, ("Under thy Protection"). The earliest text of this prayer dates from the third century:

> We fly to thy patronage, O holy Mother of God; despise not our petitions in our necessities, but deliver us always from all dangers, O glorious and blessed Virgin. Amen.

Medieval Devotion to Our Lady

After the collapse of the Roman Empire, Christianity suffered from the great decline in civilisation in the West, and it was mainly due to the Benedictine monasteries that the best of classical learning was preserved. Public Marian devotion in the Church began to grow again in the medieval period, which saw great saints such as St Bernard of Clairvaux (1090-1153), who was an outstanding devotee of Our Lady, and the main force behind the incredible expansion of the Cistercian order.

We can also see evidence of this Marian devotion in the great number of cathedrals dedicated to the Blessed Virgin all over Christendom in the Middle Ages, the high point of Catholic influence in Europe. Apart from the great cathedrals, there were also many other shrines and places of pilgrimage devoted to the Blessed Virgin in medieval Europe and beyond. These are practical examples of the great devotion to her which exercised a profound influence on culture and society at the time. In the broadest sense of the term, this was an evangelising movement, because the effect of preaching the Gospel does not remain constant for a given culture, but rather there is always a need for a continual re-evangelisation of each new generation.

At that time, most people could not read and would have received their Christian instruction from preaching, or from religious art and mystery plays. Marian ideas and imagery acted as a leaven in society: people were presented with her as a model in popular forms of entertainment and culture, and this could not fail to influence society as a whole for the better. Here again we have a Marian "evangelising" movement within medieval society.

In sum, the age of the cathedrals represents the flowering and triumph of Christianity in Europe, and it was not a coincidence this happened just at the time when there was a great upsurge in devotion to the Blessed Virgin. This was when the Church was at its most influential and so we might look to emulate this type of

Marian devotion in the future, as a way of supporting a resurgence of Christianity.

English Medieval Devotion to Our Lady

Devotion to Our Lady was very much present in medieval England. Early English Marian apparitions and shrines associated with her contributed to the idea that England was the "dowry" or special portion of Mary, a land particularly dedicated to her. Thus we have the Marian shrines such as those at Glastonbury, Evesham and particularly Walsingham, which became one of the most visited shrines in Europe. At the start of the fifteenth century, Thomas Arundel, Archbishop of Canterbury wrote that,

> We, the English, being the servants of her special inheritance and her own dowry, as we are commonly called, ought to surpass others in the warmth of our praise and devotion [to the Blessed Virgin Mary].

This text seems to indicate that this title of "The Dowry of Mary" was commonly being used for England at this time, perhaps indicating a much earlier origin for the term. An implication of all this, of course, is that England is still the Dowry of Mary, despite the effects of the Reformation and secularisation, and thus Catholics in England ought to be doing their utmost to promote devotion to Our Lady as a way of re-evangelising the country.

The Brown Scapular

Tradition had it that England was the place where the Brown Scapular, a sacramental worn around the neck, was revealed by Our Lady, to St Simon Stock, the English prior general of the Carmelite Order, on 16th July 1251. According to a long-standing tradition, she said to him: "This will be for you and for all Carmelites the privilege, that he who dies in this will not suffer eternal fire." After this apparition to St Simon, the Scapular devotion spread throughout the Church.

The Scapular promise implies that Mary will intercede to ensure that the wearer of the Scapular obtains the grace of final perseverance, that is, of dying in a state of grace, and this promise includes all Catholics who enrol in the Scapular. Over the centuries, the Scapular has been enriched with many indulgences and privileges by numerous popes, and particularly emphasised in recent times by Popes Pius XII and St John Paul II.

The Scapular devotion has thus stood the test of time, and in fact Our Lady appeared during the last Fatima apparition as Our Lady of Mount Carmel and carrying the Scapular. In addition, Sr Lucia of Fatima pointed to its importance in saying, "The Rosary and the Scapular are inseparable."

The Marian Rosary

It was during the medieval period that the Marian Rosary began to become popular in the Church. This devotion is traditionally associated with St Dominic (1170-1221), and with revelations made to him by Our Lady while he was engaged in his struggle against Albigensian heretics. St Dominic could well have preached sermons on the basics of the faith and interspersed them with "Hail Marys", thus initiating the idea of "meditating" on the mysteries surrounding the life, death and Resurrection of Christ.

A long-standing tradition in the Church sees this particular form of meditative prayer as the best form of devotion to Our Lady, and hence ultimately to God, since prayer to Mary is not an end in itself but leads to Christ. The majority of the popes from the late fifteenth century until the present have acclaimed the Rosary, which is really a prayerful Scriptural meditation with a mixture of vocal and mental prayer.

As we will see, the devout and meditative praying of the Rosary has greatly contributed to effective evangelisation, not least following heavenly interventions involving the Blessed Virgin. Thus devotion to the Rosary has been a very powerful means of evangelisation in the past, and can also help to attain the goals of the New Evangelisation.

Reformation and Catholic Reformation

The sixteenth century saw the Reformation, the great Protestant revolt against the Church, which paradoxically began the process of secularisation which has led to the present state of modern society with its materialist opposition to the very idea of God. In the process, the old medieval Catholic culture was largely destroyed, and a new culture arose, strongly influenced by Calvinism and the new humanistic ideas which had developed during the Renaissance. This movement was given added impetus in the centuries that followed by the so-called Enlightenment, and then by the French and Russian Revolutions.

But as the world became more secular, and thus moved further away from God, he responded by sending his Mother to earth to appear in various places to call people to prayer and repentance. We will look at four of the most important of these, namely, Guadalupe in 1531, the Rue de Bac in 1830, Lourdes in 1858, and Fatima in 1917.

The main religious result of the Reformation was that millions of people were lost to Catholicism in Europe, and although much ground was regained through the Catholic or Counter-Reformation, the result was a divided continent, leading ultimately to the virtual de-Christianisation of present-day Europe. But while this was happening, in the New World of North and South America, Our Lady was spearheading a great evangelising movement, which she initiated through her Guadalupe apparitions in Mexico in 1531.

Marian Apparitions and Evangelisation

The Marian Apparitions at Guadalupe in 1531

At Guadalupe, in December 1531, the Blessed Virgin appeared on a number of occasions to Juan Diego, a recently baptised adult convert (he was fifty-seven), at Tepeyac hill, near Mexico City. She told him of her love for the people of Mexico, and asked that the local bishop, Juan de Zumárraga, build a temple or church on that spot. Juan Diego was initially rebuffed by the bishop, who asked for a sign from heaven, but Our Lady met Juan Diego again and asked him to gather some miraculous, out-of-season roses, which he would find at the top of the hill, and then carry them in his rough cactus-fibre outer garment, his tilma, to the bishop. She strictly ordered him not to show the contents of the tilma to anyone on the way. Once he arrived, all present saw the wonderful image now known as Our Lady of Guadalupe which had been miraculously imprinted on the tilma.

News of the prodigy spread quickly and the result was that the Aztecs, who had been resistant to the Catholicism of their Spanish conquerors, flocked into the Church. The miraculous image has been preserved in Mexico now for nearly five centuries, although such fibre garments usually disintegrate within twenty years. The image has defied all attempts to give it a natural explanation and thus we can have confidence in the historicity of accounts of Our Lady of Guadalupe. It is thought that by 1539, almost nine million Indians had converted due to the Blessed Virgin's appearances, the image on the tilma, and the work of Franciscan missionaries, all of which combined to bring about one of the greatest evangelising movements in Church history to date. As St Juan Diego Cuauhtlatoatzin, Juan Diego was canonised by Pope St John Paul II in July 2002.

The Battles of Lepanto and Vienna

There have been a number of important historical incidents in which the praying of the Rosary, and more generally devotion to Our Lady, has played a crucial part, including the Battle of Lepanto. This took place on 7th October 1571, near Lepanto, off western Greece; a fleet of the Holy League, a coalition of southern European Catholic states, fought the main invasion fleet of the Ottoman Empire. The Pope, St Pius V, called for Catholics to pray the Rosary for success, and the Holy League won a decisive victory which prevented the invasion of Europe. Out of this victory came the Feast of the Holy Rosary, which is celebrated each year on 7th October.

A century later, there was another Ottoman attempt to conquer Europe, this time by land. Their forces penetrated as far as Vienna, where on 12th September 1683 the Battle of Vienna took place. This resulted in a victory for the Holy

Image of Our Lady of Guadalupe on the tilma, Mexico City.

Roman Empire forces in union with the Polish-Lithuanian Commonwealth, under the leadership of the Polish king John III Sobieski. Before the battle, Sobieski placed his force of eighty thousand troops - which was faced by an opposing force of one hundred and thirty thousand - under the protection of the Blessed Virgin, and attributed the victory to her. In commemoration, in 1684 Blessed Pope Innocent XI declared the Feast of the Holy Name of Mary a universal feast of the Church. It is celebrated annually on 12th September.

St John Eudes and St Louis de Montfort

On a theological and devotional level, St John Eudes (1601-1680) and St Louis de Montfort (1673-1716) did much to promote Marian devotion in France in the seventeenth and early eighteenth centuries. St John Eudes founded the Society of Jesus and Mary, and preached many missions in France, while St Louis de Montfort spent most of his priestly life preaching and teaching in western France, particularly in the Vendée area. He focussed on the principle that just as God had initiated the work of Redemption on the basis of Mary's co-operation, so he would continue and finish that work by means of her: "It was through the blessed Virgin Mary that Jesus Christ came into the world, and it is also through her that he must reign in the world."

He stressed Mary's role as spiritual mother of all Christians, basing himself on the fact of her divine maternity and her role in the Redemption. He taught that by means of her faith, trust, love, and holiness, she merited the status of "Co-Redemptrix", one that gives her rights over all mankind, since Jesus's death was sufficient to save all mankind. And so, just as a young child is totally dependent on its mother for everything, so we (or so St Louis de Montfort argued) as part of the mystical Body of Christ, are totally spiritually dependent on her and thus are her spiritual children (*True Devotion to Mary*, 25). St Louis's teaching, although not an official part of the Church's dogma, has been approved by a number of popes, and he was finally canonised in 1947.

Between the Reformation and the French Revolution destructive anti-Christian philosophies put down deep roots, as an intellectual climate innately hostile to religion developed. The French Revolution itself was a further stage in the revolt against Christendom and Catholic ideas generally, and led to the persecution of the Church in France. The western part of the country, and particularly the Vendée where St Louis de Montfort had laboured so valiantly, rose up against the revolutionaries after the king, Louis XVI, was executed; but this rising was cruelly put down.

The Apparitions at Rue de Bac in 1830

In the aftermath of the French Revolutionary excesses, Our Lady appeared to Catherine Labouré, a young novice sister of the Daughters of Charity, on 18th July 1830, in the chapel at the convent at Rue de Bac in Paris. She told Catherine that she had a mission for her, and that bad times were coming, but promised help and grace for those who prayed. In particular she spoke of the religious persecution which would break out in Paris later in the century, while also foretelling the coming revolution in the capital, which duly happened later that month.

Later in the same year, on 27th November, Catherine again saw Mary in the chapel. She was dressed in white, standing on a globe and holding a golden ball, with rings on her fingers flashing with light. An inner voice told her that the ball represented the whole world and that the rays coming from Mary's fingers represented graces for individuals. The golden ball then vanished as this apparition changed to represent Mary with her arms outstretched, inside an oval frame with the following golden lettering: "O Mary, conceived without sin, pray for us who have recourse to thee."

Again, an interior voice spoke, telling her to have a medal struck on this model. It would be a source of great graces and should be worn around the neck. Once the medal was struck and distributed, it rapidly earned the title of the "miraculous" medal. This sacramental was an important element in reviving Catholic belief in France, and also prepared the way for the proclamation of the dogma of Mary's Immaculate Conception by Blessed

Pope Pius IX in 1854. The actual name of the medal is the "Medal of the Immaculate Conception", and it played a vital role in making people more aware of the Blessed Virgin's privileged status. Catherine worked in a hostel for old men for forty years and was eventually canonised, in 1947, as St Catherine Labouré.

The Apparitions at Lourdes in 1858

The next important Marian apparitions were at Lourdes in south west France, when the Blessed Virgin initially appeared to fourteen year old Bernadette Soubirous on 11th February 1858. Bernadette saw a beautiful young girl in a niche at a rocky outcrop called Massabielle, about a half mile outside the town. She was near a wild rose bush and surrounded by a brilliant light and a golden cloud, smiling, with her arms extended towards Bernadette.

This was the beginning of a whole sequence of apparitions, eighteen in all, which occurred during the spring and early summer of 1858. Mary first spoke to Bernadette on 18th February when she asked her if she would come to the grotto for a fortnight. Thursday 25th February saw a crowd of about three hundred, and the discovery that was to make Lourdes famous, that of the miraculous spring in the grotto.

During subsequent apparitions Mary asked for a chapel and processions, but the local parish priest, Fr Peyramale, insisted that the Lady would have to reveal her name

The grotto at Massabielle where Our Lady appeared to St Bernadette.

before anything could be done. Early on 25th March, the feast of the Annunciation, Bernadette made her way to the grotto, where the beautiful Lady was already waiting for her. She asked the Lady her name; the Lady joined her hands at the breast and, looking up to heaven, said, "I am the Immaculate Conception."

The local bishop set up a Canonical Commission into the apparitions and their cause, as a growing number of cures were reported. In January 1862, he delivered his positive verdict on Lourdes in a pastoral letter, a verdict that silenced those hostile to Bernadette, who, after much suffering, died at the early age of thirty-five; she was canonised in 1933.

The Church and the Nineteenth Century Marian Revival

The various Marian apparitions which took place during the nineteenth century, and particularly in France, thus did a great deal to revive Catholicism in Europe after the negative influence of the various revolutionary outbursts, added to the ongoing secularising effects of the Reformation and Enlightenment.

Clearly the Church would have been much weaker without those interventions. Imagine if there had been no Guadalupe and the millions of conversions it prompted, thus changing the whole course of Mexican and indeed North and South American history. Or imagine if there had been no Miraculous Medal, or no apparitions to St Bernadette at Lourdes and the numerous miraculous cures at the grotto, and the huge effect these have had on Catholic life.

The role of the apparitions and miracles at Lourdes, and of St Bernadette, profoundly strengthened the Church in France in the face of nineteenth century materialism. And given France's position at the time as the "eldest daughter of the Church", that is, the most influential Catholic country, then what happened in France strongly influenced what happened in the Catholic Church generally. Thus this devotion to Our Lady was an important means of building up the Faith, which is a strong component of evangelisation.

Apart from these divine initiatives done through the Blessed Virgin, we should also remember all the religious orders dedicated to Our Lady which had been in existence for centuries, such as the Carmelites and the Servites. During the nineteenth century, there was a great growth in religious congregations, some focusing on charitable work, others on evangelisation. The Salesian Religious Institute, founded by St John Bosco and dedicated to the education of the young, is one such example. He particularly promoted devotion to Our Lady under the title Mary Help of Christians. Clearly, the combined efforts of these religious orders have had a huge impact on the Church's work of evangelisation, both in the past and still today.

The papacy at this time was also very keen to promote Marian devotion, realising that is was a bulwark against growing secularising trends in society, as the effects of the Industrial Revolution gathered pace. In the late nineteenth century, Pope Leo XIII (1878-1903) wrote numerous encyclicals on the Rosary, and urged Christians to pray it, saying: "Our need of divine help is as great today as when the great Dominic introduced the use of the Rosary of Mary as a balm for the wounds of his contemporaries." In regard to devotion to Mary generally, he said, "So great is her favour before God that whosoever in his need will not have recourse to her is trying to fly without wings," while his successor, Pope St Pius X said, "True devotion to Christ demands true devotion to Mary."

The Apparitions at Fatima in 1917

The apparitions at Fatima in Portugal, which took place between May and October 1917, can be regarded as the most important series of Marian apparitions of the twentieth century, and indeed amongst the most important events in absolute terms, particularly because of the tremendous "Miracle of the Sun" which was seen by a crowd of at least seventy thousand. Fatima is important, too, because of its connection with the papacy, and because a period of peace was promised to the world by the Blessed Virgin, provided people heeded her words.

Fatima occurred just as the Russian Revolution was unfolding in 1917, during the First World War. This revolution represented another stage in the progressive denial and rejection of God which began in earnest with the Reformation and was continued by the Enlightenment and the French Revolution. In answer to the threat represented by these successive revolutions, the Blessed Virgin appeared and asked for repentance, conversion to God, and a turning away from sin, to prevent further disasters afflicting mankind.

The essence of the Fatima Message is contained in Our Lady's words to Jacinta and Francisco Marto, and Lucia dos Santos, during the 13th June 1917 apparition at the Cova da Iria at Fatima: that Jesus wanted to use the children to make her known and loved, and that he wished to establish devotion to her Immaculate Heart throughout the world.

Fulfilling Our Lady's requests at Fatima, then, is essentially about our becoming devoted to her Immaculate Heart, to seeing her as, under God, our all-powerful spiritual mother, who came down from heaven precisely to lead her children back to God. That is the most crucial element, although her other requests, such as praying the Rosary, the Five First Saturdays devotion of reparation, and the wearing of the Brown Scapular, are also important.

During the 13th July apparition, Our Lady promised that in October she would "perform a miracle for all to see and believe." She also showed the children a vision of hell, the first part of the Fatima secret, before saying that to save them God wished to establish in the world devotion to her Immaculate Heart. If this was done many souls would be saved, but if not, then a worse war would break out involving persecutions of the Church and the Holy Father. To prevent this, she said she would come to ask for the consecration of Russia to her Immaculate Heart, and the Communion of Reparation on the First Saturdays. She also spoke of Russia spreading its errors throughout the world - communism initially, and then the ensuing godless materialism and secularism that the world is currently experiencing.

Finally, though, she said,

> In the end, my Immaculate Heart will triumph. The Holy Father will consecrate Russia to me and she will be converted, and a period of peace will be granted to the world.

Fatima More Recently

The second part of the Fatima secret was revealed in the 1940s, while the final part was revealed by Cardinal Ratzinger at the request of Pope St John Paul II in June 2000. This last part is concerned with the persecutions faced by the popes and the Church in the twentieth century. It describes how the seers saw a bishop dressed in white, which they understood was the Holy Father, with clergy and religious, going up a steep mountain which had a cross at its top, and passing through a half-ruined city. The Pope prayed for the dead on his way, much afflicted and moving slowly, but was killed at the top by soldiers, as were the clergy, religious and lay people with him.

In May 2000, in Fatima, Pope John Paul II beatified Francisco and Jacinta, who unlike Sr Lucia had died young, in 1919 and 1920, thus giving them to us as the perfect examples of how to live the Fatima message and thereby become sanctified as they did, simply by doing everything Our Lady asked of them.

To live Our Lady's message, then, is to follow a path of personal sanctification, and thus the Fatima message is exceptionally relevant for the Church in the difficult times in which we are living. If (as seems likely) they are canonised, Francisco and Jacinta will become the first non-martyr child saints in the history of the Church. Here again we have a definite link to evangelisation, since unless we make some attempt to live holy lives, our evangelising efforts are likely to bear very little fruit.

On 13th October 1917, as rain fell in torrents, at least seventy thousand people gathered at the Cova da Iria in anticipation of the miracle promised by Our Lady three months previously. At noon, the rain suddenly stopped, the clouds parted, and while the children saw various apparitions of the Holy Family, the vast crowd saw the sun gyrate in the sky for about ten minutes, sending out shafts of multi-coloured light, before plunging towards the earth. Many in the crowd thought it was the end of the

Our Lady of Fatima, Portugal.

world, but the sun then resumed its normal appearance and place in the heavens. Other people witnessed the solar miracle from a distance, which seems to rule out any type of collective hallucination. When the miracle was over, everyone's clothes and the entire Cova da Iria were dry.

The Rosary and Later Revelations to Sr Lucia

One of the things Our Lady particularly emphasised at Fatima was the Rosary. At every one of her six Fatima apparitions she specifically asked for the Rosary to be prayed. She focussed on the power of the Rosary, saying, on 13th July: "I want you to continue to pray the Rosary every day in honour of Our Lady of the Rosary, to obtain peace for the world and the end of the war." Significantly she added that they should pray this way because only she, the Lady of the Rosary, could help mankind.

Pope St John Paul II, in his homily at Fatima on 13th May 1982, said:

> The Rosary is Mary's prayer, in which…she herself prays with us. Take care of your inheritance of faith… do you want me to teach you the secret of keeping it? It is simple. Pray, pray very much, pray, recite the Rosary every day.

On 10th December 1925, the Blessed Virgin and the Child Jesus appeared to Lucia at her convent at Pontevedra in Spain, where she was a postulant in the Dorothean Order. Our Lady spoke to her about the need for reparation to her Immaculate Heart, and promised her assistance at the hour of death, with all the graces necessary for salvation, for all those who on the first Saturday of five consecutive months went to confession, received Holy Communion, and recited five decades of the Rosary, along with a quarter of an hour's meditation on the mysteries of the Rosary, with the intention of making reparation to her Immaculate Heart.

On 13th June 1929, while she was making a Holy Hour in the convent chapel at Tuy in Spain, Sr Lucia saw a vision of the Holy Trinity with Our Lady. She heard Mary speak to her:

> The moment has come in which God asks the Holy Father, in union with all the Bishops of the world, to make the consecration of Russia to my Immaculate Heart, promising to save it by this means. There are so many souls whom the Justice of God condemns for sins committed against me, that I have come to ask reparation: sacrifice yourself for this intention and pray.

These two later apparitions are important because during the July 1917 apparition, Our Lady spoke of them jointly, and so we can infer that the widespread adoption of the Five First Saturdays devotion is linked with the conversion of Russia and world peace.

Consecration of Portugal and Poland to Mary's Immaculate Heart

In 1931, the Portuguese bishops collectively consecrated Portugal to Mary's Immaculate Heart, and in 1936, at the site of the Fatima apparitions, with the prospect of the country being afflicted with communism as a result of the civil war raging in neighbouring Spain, they made a vow to organise a national pilgrimage to Fatima if Portugal was delivered from this fate. Their country was indeed preserved from communism, and as a result they were able to return in May 1938 to fulfil their vow and renew the previous consecration. They were joined by half a million ordinary Portuguese.

The fact that Portugal was able to keep out of the Second World War, in contrast to its involvement in the First World War, was to many a sign of the power of these consecrations, and of a third one made by the bishops of Portugal in the cathedral of Lisbon on 8th December 1940.

On 8th September 1946, Poland was consecrated to the Immaculate Heart of Mary at the Marian shrine at Jasna Gora in the presence of seven hundred thousand Poles. Poland was thus the first country to follow the example of Portugal in making this consecration, and we can see the fruit of this in their extraordinary resistance to communism under Cardinal Wyszynski, the election of Cardinal Wojtyła as Pope John Paul II, and the rise of the Solidarity movement in Poland following his visit in June 1979.

The important thing to note about these consecrations is that they were not just ceremonial occasions, but rather, when done with a living devotion, and invoking the intervention of God through his Mother, they had a real impact. The message for us is that if individuals, parishes, dioceses and countries make such a consecration, then they are inviting Mary to help them experience the presence of God in a decisive way in their own lives and more widely, and are thus furthering the evangelising efforts of the Church as a whole.

Our Lady and Evangelisation in Modern Times

Twentieth Century Marian Organisations

Apart from Marian apparitions, there have also been a number of Marian organisations which developed during the twentieth century and which played an important part in the process of evangelisation. These include the Militia of the Immaculate *(Militia Immaculatae)*, founded by St Maximilian Kolbe (1894-1941) in 1917; the Legion of Mary, founded by Frank Duff (1889-1980) in 1921; and the World Apostolate of Fatima, which was founded in 1947 in America as the *Blue Army of Our Lady of Fatima*.

It is worth noting that St Louis de Montfort was quite an important figure as regards the background and spirituality of both the *Militia Immaculatae* and the Legion of Mary. St Maximilian and Frank Duff took up some of the ideas in his books, *The Secret of Mary* and *True Devotion to Mary*, and advocated a total consecration to Our Lady, and thus to Christ, as a primary means of sanctification.

The *Militia Immaculatae* is now a worldwide movement for evangelisation, present in forty-six countries, and with a membership of nearly four million. It advocates total consecration to the Our Lady as the means to bring about a spiritual renewal both for individuals and for society.

The Legion of Mary is a lay Catholic organisation whose aim is the sanctification of its members through prayer, and through co-operating with Mary in working for the good of the Church. It is estimated it has over three million active members worldwide. There is a focus in the Legion on a "spiritual" apostolate, rather than material care. The whole idea of legionary service is based on the doctrine of the Mystical Body of Christ. By working with Mary, legionaries seek to serve their fellow members of the Body of Christ, and see Christ in them. Frank Duff had a broad vision for the Legion and wanted to see a particular focus on evangelisation and conversion. In particular, he emphasised the essential point that the laity have a crucial role in building up the Church, the Body of Christ. And in fact, the Legion was one of the great forces working within the Church for this end prior to the Second Vatican Council. The fact that it was able to spread all over the world from the 1930s onwards showed that it really was possible to mobilise the laity in the pursuit of evangelisation.

The Effects of Communism and Nazism

While the *Militia Immaculatae* and the Legion of Mary were slowly growing in strength, the evil effects of the Russian Revolution, as prophesied by Our Lady at Fatima, became ever more evident. The new communist state, the Soviet Union, grew in strength in succeeding years, developing its secret police and slave labour systems.

Religion was persecuted and millions imprisoned or killed in a tyranny that reached dreadful levels during the 1930s under Lenin's successor Stalin.

Communism and Nazism were the two great scourges of God and the Church during this era, and yet although in many respects they were deeply hostile to each other, both had their roots in socialist thinking and it was the threat of communism in Germany that in part made possible the success of Hitler's Nazism.

The power of the Rosary was once again dramatically shown in 1955, when the occupying Soviet Army voluntarily left the eastern zone of Austria, which as part of Germany during the Second World War, had, like Germany, been split up into four zones. Fr Petrus Pavlicek, a Franciscan, had organised a Rosary Crusade in the country from 1946 onwards, which eventually had ten percent of the population praying five decades of the Rosary daily for peace. He also organised candlelit processions in Vienna with a statue of Our Lady from Fatima.

On 15th May 1955 - two days after the Fatima anniversary day - the Soviets joined the Western Allies in signing a treaty establishing the Austrian state. All the occupying armies, including the Russians, left Austria that October. This was highly unusual; in contrast, the attempted revolutions in Hungary in 1956 and Czechoslovakia in 1968 were brutally put down by Soviet tanks.

The Rosary also played a part in saving Brazil in the 1960s and Portugal in the 1970s from communism, when national Rosary crusades were organised in both countries.

The Papacy and the Rosary during the 1950s and 1960s

During the 1950s, Pope Pius XII (1939-1958) was insistent about the power and importance of the Rosary, saying in his encyclical *Ingruentium Malorum*, which was issued in 1951,

> We do not hesitate to affirm again publicly that We put great confidence in the Holy Rosary for the healing of evils which afflict our times.

And Pius XII was, of course, the Pope who promulgated the dogma of the Assumption of Our Lady into heaven, body and soul, in 1950. This dogmatic pronouncement, and the previous one concerning the Immaculate Conception in 1854, point to Our Lady's great importance for the Church in our modern era.

Pius XII's successor, Pope St John XXIII, was particularly devoted to the Rosary, and said all fifteen decades daily. He issued an encyclical on it, *Grata Recordatio*, in 1959, in which he urged the recitation of the Rosary, particularly during the month of October.

The World Apostolate of Fatima in the 1940s and 1950s

The "Blue Army" began in the United States in 1947 as a collaboration between Mgr Harold Colgan and John Haffert. After reading that part of the Fatima message involving the conversion of Russia, Mgr Colgan asked his parishioners to form a "Blue Army" of Our Lady of Fatima, to counteract spiritually the Red Army of communism. John Haffert had met Sr Lucia and developed a Pledge Card based on the Fatima message, having previously run a society devoted to promoting the Brown Scapular.

The Pledge involved saying the Morning Offering, wearing the Brown Scapular, and praying the Rosary daily, with the Fatima Five First Saturdays devotion as an optional extra. Focussing on this Pledge, the Blue Army of Our Lady of Fatima began to rapidly expand first in the United States and then around the world. It is estimated that anywhere between thirty and forty million people have signed this Pledge.

After the collapse of communism in the former Soviet Union, the name of the organisation was changed to the "World Apostolate of Fatima" to reflect the fact that the message of Fatima is a call to conversion and repentance, as in the Gospel (*Mk* 1:15), and is addressed to every human being.

The World Apostolate of Fatima is a Public International Association of the Faithful, and as such comes under the responsibility of the Pontifical Council for the Laity. This status means that the World Apostolate can speak authoritatively and officially on behalf of the Church about the message of Fatima. Like many other Catholic organisations, the World Apostolate is experiencing great growth in the developing world, particularly in a number of African countries, in India, and in the Philippines.

Vatican II and Marian Devotion

So we have seen how devotion to Our Lady has been crucial to evangelisation in the past, and now we can look at how this has developed in more recent times, and the implications of this for her role in the future.

If we look at the documents of the Second Vatican Council, we can see aspects of them as important for the New Evangelisation, even though it has sometimes been argued that some of the texts put too much emphasis on the values present in other Christian denominations and even other religions, to the detriment of the Church's missionary impetus.

The fact that *Lumen Gentium* ("The Light of the Nations"), the Council's dogmatic Constitution of the Church, has a whole section devoted to Our Lady, rather than dealing with her in a separate document, invites us to understand the importance of her role at the heart of the Church, and to realise that Marian devotion and action are not just optional extras.

At the close of the third session of the Council, on 21st November 1964, Blessed Pope Paul VI proclaimed Mary as "Mother of the Church". His apostolic exhortation *Signum Magnum* ("A Great Sign") was issued on 13th May 1967, the fiftieth anniversary of the first Fatima apparition and the occasion of his one-day pilgrimage to Fatima: the first by a reigning pope. Fatima was also specifically mentioned in the document. In his apostolic exhortation *Recurrens Mensis Octobris*, issued on 7th October 1969, the Pope urged Catholics to deepen their devotion to the Rosary.

Recent Popes, Our Lady, and the New Evangelisation

Popes since Vatican II on the New Evangelisation

Marialis Cultus ("Marian Devotion") is the title of a Mariological apostolic letter written by Blessed Pope Paul VI and issued on 2nd February 1974. It is subtitled "For the Right Ordering and Development of Devotion to the Blessed Virgin Mary", and focusses on Marian liturgical celebrations, and the Angelus and Rosary. It was influenced by the Second Vatican Council's Constitution on the Sacred Liturgy - *Sacrosanctum Concilium* - and also by Chapter Eight of *Lumen Gentium*. In this letter, the Pope wanted to respond to a perceived Marian "crisis" that had arisen following the Council, in which Marian devotion was being downplayed by some in the Church.

The liturgical focus of *Marialis Cultus* illustrates an important but often overlooked point regarding the feast days and solemnities assigned to the Blessed Virgin in the liturgy. These include the Solemnity of Mary, Mother of God (1st January), the Annunciation (25th March), the Assumption (15th August), the Immaculate Conception (8th December), and the feast days associated with Christmas. And we could also add the particular Marian feast days associated with approved Marian apparitions, such as Our Lady of Lourdes (11th February), Our Lady of Fatima (13th May), and Our Lady of Guadalupe (12th December).

If we follow the ancient maxim *lex orandi, lex credendi* ("the law of prayer is the law of belief"), then this prominence given to Mary in the liturgy, which is the supreme form of prayer in the Church, ought to be reflected in our beliefs and practices. And if the liturgy should be at the centre of deep Catholic reform and evangelisation, and Our Lady's feasts are so prominent in it, then her role must be far more important than is generally recognised.

The Synod of Bishops discussed evangelisation in 1974; in his Post-Synodal Apostolic Exhortation *Evangelii Nuntiandi* (1975), Blessed Pope Paul VI said: "The Church exists in order to evangelise, that is, to preach and teach, to be the channel of the gift of grace" (par.14). The Pope stressed that Catholics ought to be willing to witness about their faith to their fellow men and women, ultimately with a view to bringing about an inner change in their lives leading to their conversion.

Pope St John Paul II, the Rosary, and Fatima

Even before St John Paul II became Pope in 1978, he had adopted the Latin phrase "Totus Tuus" as his episcopal motto, as an expression of his personal consecration to Our Lady following the example of St Louis de Montfort, whose writings he had studied closely as a young man.

Throughout his pontificate, the Pope did what he could to spread devotion to the Blessed Virgin, by means of his encyclicals, pastoral letters, general audiences and homilies, realising that an understanding of her role was vital if the New Evangelisation he was promoting was to be a success.

He was also very keen to promote the Rosary, and issued his own Apostolic Letter on it, *Rosarium Virginis Mariae*, in 2002. In this, amongst other things, he acknowledged how devoted he was to the Rosary, and noted how many of his predecessors had attributed great importance to it. He also wrote:

> The Rosary, reclaimed in its full meaning, goes to the very heart of Christian life; it offers a familiar yet fruitful spiritual and educational opportunity for personal contemplation, the formation of the People of God, and the new evangelisation." (par. 3)

He proclaimed the year from October 2002 to October 2003 the "Year of the Rosary", and instituted the new "Mysteries of Light". Following the failed assassination attempt on 13th May 1981, and his subsequent recovery, in thanksgiving he visited Fatima in 1982. During his homily, the Pope said:

> If the Church has accepted the message of Fatima, it is above all because that message contains a truth and a call whose basic content is the truth and call of the Gospel itself.

He further stated that "the appeal of the Lady of the message of Fatima is so deeply rooted in the Gospel and the whole of Tradition that the Church feels that the message imposes a commitment on her."

Later on, the Pope credited Our Lady with saving his life, saying, "One hand fired the shot, another guided it." It is worth pondering what would have happened if he had died in May 1981: in essence, we would have been deprived of over two decades more of his inspired teaching and example, which would have been a great loss to the Church.

The Collegial Consecration Explained

All the popes since Pius XII have strongly approved of Fatima, but it was actually Pope St John Paul II who fulfilled Our Lady's request for the collegial consecration, when, on 25th March 1984, he carried out the consecration in Rome in the presence of the statue of Our Lady from the Capelinha in Fatima. Following this consecration, Sr Lucia, who was now a Carmelite at Coimbra in Portugal, was visited by the Apostolic Nuncio, and she confirmed that the consecration of Russia had indeed been accomplished, and that God had accepted it.

In Russia, after the death of Konstantin Chernenko, Mikhail Gorbachev succeeded him on 11th March 1985 as General Secretary of the Communist Party. Gorbachev became President in 1988, and began the process which led to the collapse of communism in Eastern Europe and

Pope St John Paul II.

the peaceful dissolution of the Soviet Union. We can say Pope St John Paul II's collegial consecration terminated the persecution of the Church in Eastern Europe, and opened the way for its resurrection. The power of the Fatima message is certainly evident in the huge changes that have taken place in Russia and its former satellites since 1984. But although the power of communism has been largely broken, its inner essence, its atheistic ideology, which is based on pure materialism, has continued to evolve, and has now become a worldwide phenomenon, one which is actively working to remove what is left of Christian morality from the public domain.

After a century, then, the message of Fatima still retains its importance and relevance, and since the Blessed Virgin specifically returned and appeared to Sr Lucia to speak about the Five First Saturdays devotion in 1925, this devotion surely needs to be practised much more widely in the Church as a form of re-evangelisation. This will bring Catholics to live their faith more fully through regular reception of the sacraments of Confession and the Eucharist, with the assurance of Our Lady's promise to assist them at the hour of death "with all the graces necessary for salvation." Widespread adoption of the First Saturdays devotion should be a major part of the New Evangelisation, with the particular aim of reviving the Church in the West.

Pope St John Paul II on Evangelisation, Renewal and Holiness

Pope St John Paul II promoted the New Evangelisation strongly during his pontificate, and in 1983 spoke of the need for the Church to be new in its ardour, methods and expression, with the implication that the way the Church was passing on the Gospel message - that is, evangelising - was not working as it should, and so a new approach was needed, one that would have much more of an impact on our "post-Christian" society, with a particular focus on personal holiness.

The Pope was, of course, also a great champion of marriage and the family, and believed that the family had a very important role to play in the New Evangelisation, to the extent that if it could be renewed in a Christian sense, then it could act powerfully to change both secular culture and the world as a whole, and thus help to establish a new "civilisation of love." We can find his views on this topic most cogently expressed in his apostolic exhortation *Familiaris Consortio*, which was issued in November 1981. Here, he boldly stated that, "The future of the world and of the Church passes through the family" (par.170), having previously said that "the future of evangelisation depends in great part on the Church of the home" (par.124). Thus he closely associated the spiritual health of the family with the New Evangelisation.

Redemptoris Mater

Pope St John Paul II's encyclical letter *Redemptoris Mater* ("The Mother of the Redeemer"), which was issued on 25th March 1987, focusses on the Blessed Virgin in relation to her Son and his Church, and is regarded as a landmark in reinvigorating Marian devotion and theology amongst Catholics. In it, the Pope mentioned St Louis de Montfort as one of the vital influences on his Marian thinking. The letter is divided into three main parts. The first looks at Mary in terms of the mystery of Christ, while the second part deals with Mary's role as the Mother of God within the pilgrim Church, and the third part focusses on Mary's maternal mediation.

Apart from this, in his general audiences between September 1995 and November 1997, the Pope delivered seventy talks on the Blessed Virgin Mary, thus providing a powerful series of catecheses on the role and importance of Our Lady for Catholics worldwide.

Christifideles Laici

In his Apostolic Exhortation *Christifideles Laici* on the Vocation and Mission of the Lay Faithful, issued on 30th December 1988, Pope St John Paul II devoted several paragraphs to the subject of holiness (pars. 16, 17), which he said was "the prime and fundamental vocation" of the lay faithful, citing the Extraordinary Synod of Bishops in 1985, which declared that "today we have the greatest need of saints whom we must assiduously beg God to raise up" (par. 16).

Following this, the Pope issued an encyclical on missionary activity, *Redemptoris Missio* ("The Mission of thc Redeemer"), in December 1990. In this he emphasised that Jesus Christ is the only Saviour, that the Holy Spirit is the principal agent of the whole of the Church's mission, and that the Church as a whole is meant to have a missionary focus, given that the horizons for missionary activity today are so vast, since so many millions of people do not know Christ.

In his conclusion, the Pope focussed on the role of the Blessed Virgin, saying:

> We too, like the apostles, need to be transformed and guided by the Spirit. ...Mary is the model of that maternal love which should inspire all who co-operate in the Church's apostolic mission for the rebirth of humanity. (par. 92)

In his apostolic letter *Novo Millennio Ineunte*, issued in 2001, Pope St John Paul II, discussed the importance and necessity of the New Evangelisation, and described the Blessed Virgin as the "Star of the New Evangelisation", having previously entrusted the Third Millennium to her at the Jubilee Mass on 8th October 2000.

In June 2003, the Pope issued his Post-Synodal Apostolic Exhortation *Ecclesia in Europa* ("The Church in Europe").

This discusses the signs of hope, and the challenges facing the Church on that continent. He concluded by entrusting the future of both the Church in Europe and its citizens to the Blessed Virgin, saying, "The whole Church…looks to Mary" (par. 124). He also said:

> Church in Europe! Continue to contemplate Mary, in the knowledge that she is "maternally present and sharing in the many complicated problems which today beset the lives of individuals, families, and nations.

Pope Benedict XVI, Fatima, and the New Evangelisation

Pope Benedict XVI issued a call for evangelisation and holiness on his visit to Fatima in May 2010. In his address to the bishops of Portugal he said:

> The times in which we live demand a new missionary vigour on the part of Christians, who are called to form a mature laity, identified with the Church and sensitive to the complex transformations taking place in our world…[in this situation] what is decisive is the ability to inculcate in all those engaged in the work of evangelisation a true desire for holiness, in the awareness that the results derive above all from our union with Christ and the working of the Holy Spirit.

Pope Benedict made a number of notable pronouncements at Fatima, the most important of which was his declaration, on 13th May 2010, that it was "mistaken to think that Fatima's prophetic mission is complete."

Pope Benedict was insistent, too, in warning about the dangers of an aggressive secularism which seeks to drive religion out of society completely, and is thus a real threat to religious liberty. He likewise warned about a relativism which sees all beliefs as equally valid, and thus denies objective truth, and which leads to a "dictatorship of relativism", in which all that matters for individuals are their own egotistical desires. The remedy he saw for all this was a New Evangelisation which would put forward a convincing alternative Christian vision of man and society.

To this end, as indicated above, in 2010 he created a new Pontifical Council, the Council for Promoting New Evangelisation, saying its task was to promote

> a renewed evangelisation in countries where the first proclamation of the faith [had] already resounded, and where Churches are present of ancient foundation, but which are going through a progressive secularisation of society and a sort of "eclipse of the sense of God", which constitutes a challenge to find the appropriate means to propose again the perennial truth of the Gospel of Christ.

Overall, then, we can say that what has happened in recent years is that we have witnessed a progressive de-Christianisation of Western society, a process which is accelerating with worrying rapidity under the influence of a secular media which is obsessed with money, fame, and sex, and a technological impetus which increasingly pays no heed to previous moral boundaries. Thus a New Evangelisation, and one which has a strong Marian element, is imperative for the Church if these trends are to be countered.

Pope Francis, Our Lady, and the New Evangelisation

Pope Francis has also promoted the Marian dimension of Catholicism during his pontificate. He has shown himself to be very supportive of Fatima, and indeed he arranged for his pontificate to be consecrated to Our Lady of Fatima on 13th May 2013 by the Cardinal Patriarch of Lisbon and the bishops of Portugal, on the ninety-sixth anniversary of the first apparition of Our Lady at Fatima.

It is also significant that the Marian Day in Rome for the Year of Faith was centred on Fatima, and was celebrated on 12th-13th October 2013, the anniversary of Our Lady's final apparition at Fatima, and of the Miracle of the Sun. The Pope presided at the ceremonies in the presence of her statue, which was brought to St Peter's from Fatima, and entrusted the world to Mary. These events show that Pope Francis has maintained the close links between the papacy and Fatima.

And we can see how he views the importance of the role of Mary in the New Evangelisation given that in his

Pope Francis in St Peter's Square at the Vatican.

apostolic exhortation *Evangelii Gaudium* ("The Joy of the Gospel") there is a section entitled "Mary, mother of evangelisation" (pars. 284-288), in which the Pope states that there "is a Marian 'style' to the Church's work of evangelisation." He also wrote that Mary "is the Mother of the Church which evangelises, and without her we could never truly understand the spirit of the new evangelisation" (par. 284). Pope Francis also wrote:

> We ask the Mother of the living Gospel to intercede that this invitation to a new phase of evangelisation will be accepted by the entire ecclesial community…Today we look to her and ask her to help us proclaim the message of salvation to all and to enable new disciples to become evangelisers in turn…We implore her intercession… that the way may be opened to the birth of a new world (pars. 287, 288).

And Pope Francis prayed as follows to Our Lady in his conclusion to *Evangelii Gaudium*:

"Star of the new evangelisation, help us to bear radiant witness to communion, service, ardent and generous faith, justice and love of the poor, that the joy of the Gospel may reach to the ends of the earth…"

Here, then, the Pope is in effect putting the Blessed Virgin at the forefront of the New Evangelisation, and so the challenge for the Church is how to translate that vision into reality.

Our Lady and the New Evangelisation, Now and in the Future

Movements inspired by love for Mary have been very active agents of the New Evangelisation, and we can see a strong element of Marian devotion in many of the new movements and communities which have grown up in the Church, particularly since the Second Vatican Council. But as already mentioned, some essentially lay movements, such as the Legion of Mary, Opus Dei, and the Knights of Our Lady (*Militia Sanctae Mariae*), were active long before that. And it has also been said of many of these new movements that they have three main characteristics, namely a strong focus on the Eucharist, on the papacy, and on devotion to Mary.

New Movements

The Foyers de Charité are communities headed by a priest, but made up of lay members, who have a strong devotion to Mary, as did their co-foundress, Marthe Robin, and there are many other such movements, including the Focolare Movement (also known as the "Work of Mary"), Communion and Liberation, the Heralds of the Gospel, the Emmanuel Community, and the Madonna House Apostolate, all of which have a Marian dimension.

Youth 2000 is a youth movement founded in Britain, but which has now spread to many countries overseas, and this has a strong evangelising impetus which includes promotion of devotion to Our Lady. The Faith Movement is another British organisation which promotes both the New Evangelisation and devotion to the Blessed Virgin. And there is an annual Pro-life Pilgrimage to Walsingham, which carries an image of Our Lady of Guadalupe, who as patroness of the unborn is increasingly seen as a pro-life symbol, since the girdle she wore during the apparitions, and which was reproduced on the tilma, is symbolic of her being with child.

There have also been specific evangelising initiatives started in Britain, including the School of the Annunciation at Buckfast Abbey, which is described as a Centre for the New Evangelisation. It offers a range of courses in key areas of the Catholic faith, and presents the teachings of the magisterium of the Church as they are rooted in Scripture and tradition. Another example of this is the St Patrick's Evangelisation School course (SPES), which takes place at St Patrick's church in Soho, London, and is a nine-month course designed to form young adults in the Catholic faith.

Practical Aspects of Marian Devotion and the New Evangelisation

In a practical sense, the best way for individuals to promote the Marian dimension of the New Evangelisation is to become involved in some way in promoting devotion to Our Lady, or living out that devotion in their own life. So at a parish or school level, it is possible to join in praying the Rosary, or start a Rosary group, or initiate a shrine or "Mary Garden" at a suitable place within a parish or school. Individuals can also join Marian organisations such as the World Apostolate of Fatima, the *Militia Immaculatae* or the Legion of Mary.

Many parishes and dioceses organise pilgrimages to Marian shrines and these can have a very potent effect on those who take part. Pope St John Paul II initiated the World Youth Days, which are normally celebrated every three years in a different country, and have grown to be powerful agents of evangelisation involving large numbers of young people. The World Youth Day Cross has been carried around the world continuously since 1984, and it is always accompanied by an icon of the Blessed Virgin Mary, to symbolise the intimate and enduring link between Christ and his Mother.

Clearly, too, the internet and the various forms of social media have become powerful means of evangelisation for the Church. But we should remember that while such methods, and also passing on the Faith through one-to-one contact through the positive Christian influence of one soul on another, are very important, Our Lord did send the apostles to teach all nations, and therefore teaching is also of the essence of evangelisation.

Ecumenism and Evangelisation

At Fatima, Our Lady said that in the end her Immaculate Heart would triumph; this triumph implies a great increase in devotion to Our Lady throughout the world. Thus the outreach which is part of the New Evangelisation means that the person and role of the Blessed Virgin within Catholicism needs to be part of the approach made by the Church to Orthodox Christians, Anglicans, Evangelicals, Jews, Muslims, and even atheists.

Clearly, the fact that the Fatima message mentions Russia, and thus is presumably related in some way to the reunion of the Catholic and Orthodox Churches, in itself indicates an important avenue of approach to the Orthodox world, as does the fact that there is a great devotion to the Blessed Virgin within the Orthodox Churches.

Many Anglicans, too, have a great devotion to Our Lady, and indeed, the new Ordinariate established in recent years for those Anglicans in England and Wales wishing to enter into full communion with the Church is officially entitled "The Personal Ordinariate of Our Lady of Walsingham". There is also an Anglican organisation entitled the "Ecumenical Friends of Fatima Association".

Evangelising Evangelicals, Jews, Muslims and Atheists

It also ought to be possible to persuade Evangelical Christians that devotion to Mary is biblically-based and thus central to a real relationship with Christ. For example, when, at the meeting between Our Lady and Elizabeth (the Visitation), Mary responded with her Magnificat, she said, "henceforth all generations will call me blessed" (*Lk* 1:48). Thus the Bible tells us that all mankind, and certainly all Christians, should be honouring Mary by calling her blessed, and not ignoring her or downplaying her importance.

Moreover, Fatima should also have an appeal for Jewish people, since Sr Lucia reported seeing a star near the bottom of Our Lady's tunic at Fatima, and this has been linked with the Old Testament story of Queen Esther, whose name means "star". She intervened to save the Jewish people on the thirteenth of the month, just as Mary appeared at Fatima on the thirteenth day of each month between May and October 1917. And this is obviously quite apart from the fact that the Blessed Virgin was Jewish, and so has a special love and concern for the Jewish people.

Regarding Islam, it is surely of significance that Fatima received its name following the Muslim occupation of Portugal. And since there is a definite and quite noteworthy place given to Blessed Virgin in the Qur'an, then devotion to Our Lady ought to be of great importance in reaching out to the Muslim world.

Fatima also ought to appeal to atheists and non-believers just as much today as it did at the time of the Miracle of the Sun, a miracle which simply cannot be explained in natural terms, and the same can be said for the miracles that have taken place at Lourdes, and the image on the Guadalupe tilma.

So, far from being a handicap in ecumenical approaches or evangelisation, devotion to the Blessed Virgin can be seen very positively.

The Future of the Marian Dimension of the New Evangelisation

In sum, it is not an exaggeration to say that Our Lady, either personally in her apparitions, or through her influence via religious orders or lay organisations, or on a cultural level, has been at the forefront of efforts to promote and expand the Church down through the centuries, which of course is the essence of evangelisation.

Regarding the future of the New Evangelisation and how it is going to be carried out and happen, St Louis de Montfort wrote, in the early eighteenth century, of the "great saints of the latter times," who by their word and example, "will draw all men to a true devotion to her." (*True Devotion*, par. 48).

As to when this will happen, he went on to say:

> When will souls breathe Mary as the body breathes air? When that time comes wonderful things will happen on earth. The Holy Spirit, finding his dear Spouse present again in souls, will come down into them with great power…[but] that day will dawn only when the devotion I teach is understood and put into practice. (par. 217)

He stated, too, that:

> If then, as is certain, the knowledge and the kingdom of Jesus Christ must come into the world, it can only be as a necessary consequence of the knowledge and reign of Mary. She who first gave him to the world will establish his kingdom in the world. (par. 13)

Thus St Louis prophesied a great Marian era to come in the future, but indicated that this will not come about unless people have a true devotion to the Blessed Virgin. In other words, the New Evangelisation must have a strong Marian element in order to be truly effective, which is also essentially what Our Lady said at Fatima.

More recently, St Maximilian Kolbe, the great martyr of Auschwitz, summed up the situation succinctly when he said that mankind "will find true happiness only when Mary Immaculate reigns over the whole world."

And indeed, Pope St John Paul II himself said in *Crossing the Threshold of Hope*: "Christ will conquer through [Mary], because he wants the Church's victories now and in the future to be linked to her."

Conclusion

The time has come for Catholics to rediscover a genuine Marian devotion, as contained in the words of recent popes, messages from approved Marian apparitions, the work of the various Marian apostolates, and the teaching of saints such as St Louis de Montfort, so as to provide a renewed impetus for the Church's evangelisation efforts. Such a devotion can supply a theme to support and inspire the New Evangelisation, as has happened so often in the past. When enough Catholics do this, then we will enter upon a time of true evangelisation and ultimately world peace, as promised by Our Lady at Fatima: "In the end, my Immaculate Heart will triumph…and a period of peace will be granted to the world."

Some Marian Prayers

Morning Offering Prayer

This prayer can be said each morning, as a way of fulfilling the request of Our Lady of Fatima that we sanctify our daily duties.

O my God, in union with the Immaculate Heart of Mary *(here kiss your Brown Scapular)*, I offer thee the Precious Blood of Jesus from all the altars throughout the world, joining with it the offering of my every thought, word and action of this day. O my Jesus, I desire today to gain every indulgence and merit I can and I offer them, together with myself, to Mary Immaculate that she may best apply them to the interests of thy most Sacred Heart. Precious Blood of Jesus, save us! Immaculate Heart of Mary, pray for us! Sacred Heart of Jesus, have mercy on us!

Consecration to the Immaculate Heart of Mary

Virgin Mary, Mother of God and our Mother, to your Immaculate Heart we consecrate ourselves, in an act of total entrustment to the Lord. By you we will be led to Christ. By him and with him we will be led to the Father. We will walk in the light of faith, and we will do everything so that the world may believe that Jesus Christ is the One sent by the Father. With him we wish to carry his love and salvation to the ends of the earth. Under the protection of your Immaculate Heart, we will be one people with Christ. We will be witnesses of his Resurrection. By him we will be led to the Father, for the glory of the Most Holy Trinity, whom we adore, praise and bless forever. Amen.

Hail Holy Queen

Hail, holy Queen, Mother of mercy, hail, our life, our sweetness and our hope. To thee do we cry, poor banished children of Eve: to thee do we send up our sighs, mourning and weeping in this vale of tears. Turn then, most gracious Advocate, thine eyes of mercy toward us and, after this our exile, show unto us the blessed fruit of thy womb, Jesus, O clement, O loving, O sweet Virgin Mary!

V. Pray for us, O holy Mother of God.

R. That we may be made worthy of the promises of Christ.

Memorare

Remember, O most gracious Virgin Mary, that never was it known that anyone who fled to thy protection, implored thy help, or sought thy intercession, was left unaided. Inspired by this confidence I fly unto thee, O Virgin of virgins, my Mother. To thee do I come, before thee I stand, sinful and sorrowful. O Mother of the Word Incarnate, despise not my petitions, but in thy mercy hear and answer me. Amen.

Practical Aspects of Devotion to Our Lady

Many Catholic spiritual writers have maintained that one of the most important prayers we should say is the Morning Offering. They stress that this should be prayed slowly and with full advertence to the meaning of the words, and that by it we offer up all our thoughts, words, deeds and sufferings to the Sacred Heart of Jesus through the Immaculate Heart of Mary, while also expressing a desire to gain all the indulgences we can. In this way we sanctify the whole day, and we can also say a daily prayer of personal consecration to Our Lady.

Even if we do not pray the official prayers of the Church, such as Morning and Evening Prayer as found in the breviary, it is still possible to say some of the prayers from the Little Office of Our Lady, which as its name indicates has a particular focus on the Blessed Virgin.

Another important Marian prayer which can be prayed daily is the Angelus; the custom of saying it dates back to the thirteenth century. This prayer focusses on the words of the angel Gabriel to Our Lady at the Annunciation, her response, and the Incarnation of Christ in her womb. It is said three times a day, in the morning on rising, at noon, and at 6 pm, and although it doesn't take long to say it properly, this is an excellent way of focussing on

Our Lady for brief periods during the day, as a way of recalling the importance of her role in salvation history.

As for the Rosary, it may be enough to say that Our Lady at Fatima specifically asked Catholics to pray the Rosary daily to bring about peace in the world, and also because it is the pre-eminent way of being more closely united with her, since she is the spiritual mother of all Christians. Saying five decades of the Rosary daily is thus an excellent way of ensuring her protection, and it is a practice which has been recommended over the centuries by many popes.

Likewise, the wearing of the Brown Scapular has a long tradition of support in the Church, and again is a sign of Our Lady's support and protection for the individual during life and even more so after death, with its great promise of avoiding the pains of hell. It is also a sign of our personal consecration to her Immaculate Heart.

The Miraculous Medal is another important sacramental of the Church, which has proved its efficacy repeatedly over the years. Again, by wearing it, the person puts themselves under the particular protection of Our Lady, and obtains many special graces.

The Fatima Five First Saturdays devotion is a very valuable way of also ensuring Our Lady's protection, and of benefitting from the regular reception of the sacrament of confession, while also being involved in the practice of reparation to her Immaculate Heart.

St Louis de Montfort's *True Devotion* is a method of total consecration to Our Lady, which starts from the fact that, as members of the mystical Body of Christ, we are her spiritual children who should do everything through, with, in and for the Blessed Virgin, as the perfect way of fulfilling our baptismal vows. His books *True Devotion to Mary* and *The Secret of Mary* explain what is involved.

Apart from the above, spiritual writers have also frequently expressed the importance of reading some chapters from the Bible daily, and also of doing some regular spiritual reading; also prayer before the Blessed Sacrament, perhaps for an hour a week, has a very important part to play in our spiritual lives.

Further Reading/References

Carol, Juniper Benjamin OFM, *Mariology*, 3 volumes. (Milwaukee, The Bruce Publishing Company, 1955-57)

Sheen, Fulton J., *The World's First Love*. (San Francisco, Ignatius Press, 2010)

O'Carroll, Michael, *Theotokos: A Theological Encyclopedia of the Blessed Virgin Mary*. (Eugene, Wipf and Stock, 2000)

Johnston, Francis, *Fatima: the Great Sign*. (Rockford, TAN Books, 2009)

Dirvin, Joseph I., *Saint Catherine Labouré of the Miraculous Medal*. (Rockford, TAN Books, 1981)

Laurentin, René, *The Life of Catherine Labouré*. (New York, Collins, 1983)

Johnston, Francis, *The Wonder of Guadalupe*. (Rockford, TAN Books, 1993)

Carroll, Warren Hasty, *Our Lady of Guadalupe and the Conquest of Darkness*. (Front Royal, Christendom Press, 1983)

Foley, Donal Anthony, *Marian Apparitions, the Bible, and the Modern World*. (Leominster, Gracewing, 2002)

Tindal-Robertson, Timothy, *Fatima, Russia and Pope John Paul II*. (Leominster, Gracewing, 1998)

Kondor, Louis, *Fatima in Lucia's own words*. (Fatima, Secretariado dos Pastorinhos, 2003)

Marchi, John de, *Fatima from the beginning*. (Fatima, Missoes Consolata, 2000)

Martins, Antonio Maria SJ & Fox, Robert Joseph, *Documents on Fatima*. (Fatima, Fatima Family Apostolate, 1992)

Pontifical Council for the promotion of the New Evangelisation: *www.vatican.va/roman_curia/pontifical_councils/new-evangelization/index.htm*

Walsingham shrine: *www.walsingham.org.uk/romancatholic/*

Glastonbury shrine: *www.glastonburyshrine.co.uk/*

Fatima Sanctuary: *www.santuario-fatima.pt/portal/?lang=EN*

Pontifical Council for the Laity: *www.laici.va/content/laici/en.html*

World Apostolate of Fatima: *www.worldfatima.com/en*

World Apostolate of Fatima England and Wales: *www.worldfatima-englandwales.org.uk/*

Militia Immaculatae: *www.militia-immaculatae.info/pages/en home.php*

Legion of Mary: *www.legionofmary.ie/*

Message of Guadalupe

Gillian Rae

Our Lady of Guadalupe, Queen of Mexico, Mother of the Americas and Protectress of the Unborn Child.Why, in 1531, did Our Lady appear to an illiterate Mexican worker, Juan Diego? How can interest and devotion to her today be so widespread? Our Lady appeared as an Indian girl, speaking Juan Diego's own native language, and offered her help to the oppressed and largely pagan people from which he came. The miraculous image, which appeared as a result on Diego's clothing, can still be seen in Mexico today. This booklet tells the story, and the message Guadalupe has for the modern world.

D652 ISBN 978 1 86082 098 4

A Simple Rosary Book

Revised by Donal Foley

Enriched by the history, customs and scripture that surround the Holy Rosary, many today are rediscovering this prayer which lies at the heart of Catholic spirituality. Through 'this school of prayer' (St John Paul II) disciples grow in love for Christ through Mary, mother of the Lord.

Designed for those familiar with the prayer as well as for newcomers, this text clearly explains how to pray the Rosary. Prayers and Scripture passages associated with the Rosary are also included.

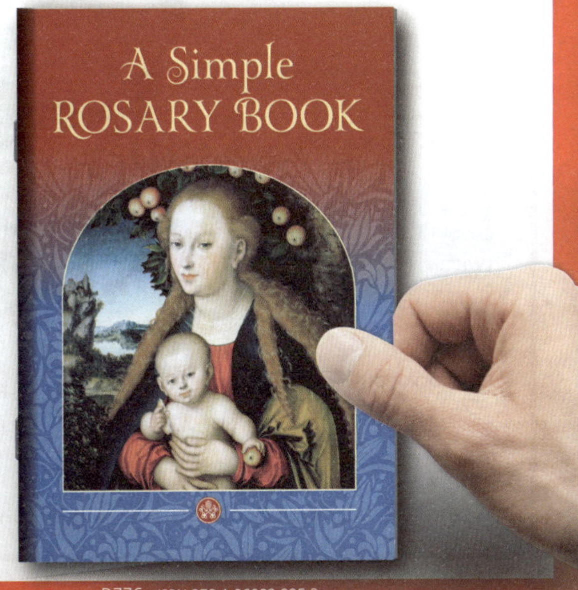

D776 ISBN 978 1 86082 925 3